Urine-Therapy

It May Save Your Life!

by

Dr. Beatrice Bartnett

Chiropractic and Naturopathic Physician

Published by the

Lifestyle Institute
P.O. Box 4735
Ruidoso, NM 88345

Other books published by this author

Auricular Therapy - Theory and Practice

by Dr. Beatrice Bartnett
This easy to use manual is for the professional acupuncturist. It contains all the points, and explains their connections and positions. There are many combinations included for treatment of diseases diagnosed by western medicine.

The Key to the Ear

by Dr. Beatrice Bartnett
The Key to the Ear is a great and easy to read, "how-to" book for the lay person. It contains information about the ear and the basic 12 Step Ear Massage program. A total of 65 illustrations on the points position as well as how to stimulate them, and an index that covers more than 140 conditions are all part of this special book.

The Miracles of Urine-Therapy

by Dr. Beatrice Bartnett and Margie Adelman
This book explains the practical applications of Urine-Therapy and gives an overview of the origin of this sacred elixir. Information on nutrition and a healthy lifestyle is also included. (Out of print)

Peace Labyrinth - Sacred Geometry

Dr. Beatrice Bartnett
This book explains how the Peace Labyrinth came about and how it can be a tool for inner guidance, as well as for physical, emotional and spiritual healing. The book will guide the reader through a full ceremony.

Books are available through the Lifestyle Institute.

A Special Dedication

to

Jeff Palladino

A
Tireless
Promoter and Researcher
of
Urine-Therapy
and a
Caring Friend.

DID YOU SAY
URINE-THERAPY?

Yes, you are right, we are talking about Urine-Therapy!

You never heard about it? I am surprised. So many people tell me their own personal stories of their European grandmother, or the Russian woman they met a long time ago, or the South American immigrant who told them to use their own urine to rid themselves of a health problem. Mostly they just laughed about it. Their feelings went out to those they thought rather "primitive" people and their quackery until one day, after many visits to different doctors, tired of trying out new salves and pills, they were encouraged to try out this very unorthodox remedy. After all, it is free!

With disbelief and amazement they could soon see and feel improvements. Their problems usually cleared up within a few days.

Did those so-thought "primitive" people know something more than our highly educated medical establishment? Of course one does not usually talk about such an experience. Who likes to be laughed at, or at least not taken seriously?

My friend, you are not alone. Thousands of people have had a similar experience. This booklet has been written for you. It gives you medical and scientific facts. Urine-Therapy – as you know – works! This booklet tells you why. If you'd like to share your personal urine story with me, please feel free to write me. God bless you.

WHAT'S IT ALL ABOUT?

Urine-Therapy is a very ancient and drugless form of intrinsic medicine. Its application is so simple that it can be done anywhere and any time. And best of all, anybody can afford the cost of the therapy. It is FREE.

Urine has been used as a healing agent in practically all civilizations and cultures. It seemingly dies only to reappear again time after time. Often it is called the Water of Life, Living Water Within, or simply Life Elixir. In many religions it is believed that this water will enhance one's spiritual growth and even give one everlasting life.[1]

In this booklet we will address more the medical and scientific facts of the therapy. Vast information on the spiritual and emotional aspects of Urine-Therapy can be found in the book *Miracles of Urine-Therapy.*

Drinking one's urine is a tool of survival. When lost in a boat on the world's ocean, or if the quality of water is uncertain, ingesting urine is the safest practice. Many soldiers have survived long periods in the wilderness thanks to this knowledge. During earthquakes and floods the drinking water often gets contaminated. Ingesting it would cause disease and many more unnecessary deaths. Urine is the answer to these problems. One may say it is better to use water pills (chlorine) to disinfect the water. The fact is that it is very difficult to reach many of the affected areas during catastrophic conditions.

Any time there is a drinking water shortage, urine is the best alternative. It does not just satisfy one's liquid intake – it actually keeps one healthy. During Jordan's Nine-Day War, The Red Crescent (the Arab counterpart of the Red Cross) raised the grim specter of massive health hazards in Amman. "Your children are expiring of thirst," said one Red Crescent radio broadcast. "We cannot help you except by telling you that you may be able to save their lives be letting them drink their own urine. It will cause them no harm."[2]

Urine may save many lives during an emergency, but more than that, it is renowned for its very strong healing properties. Urine has healed thousands of patients suffering from leprosy to cancer and even AIDS. It is believed that any disease except those caused by trauma or structural defects can be healed by this one means. How is that possible? This book will give you the facts.

2

Food for Thought

Did you know that:

1. Urine-Therapy is the most primitive, primordial and simple form of homeopathy that exists.

2. Urine-Therapy is also called "the mother of ayurvedic medicine."

3. In the days of the Roman Empire, urine was so important that according to Suetonius, the emperor placed a tax on every drop that was collected in public reservoirs! Urine had many applications, especially in the leather tanning and textile industries.[3]

4. In China, all possible bodily secretions are used as medicaments.[4]

5. In India, leprosy is put into total remission by the addition of small quantities of the patient's urine in the daily morning orange juice![5]

6. Your **own** urine is the perfect **antidote** for poisons, chemicals, and snake or animal bites![6]

7. In the 18th century, the French and Germans used cow's urine medically to help control and cure jaundice, rheumatism, gout, dropsy (edema, swelling), sciatica and asthma![7]

8. In Germany in the 1940s, doctors gave urine enemas to children exposed to measles and chicken pox. Those receiving the enemas got a much milder form of the disease![8,9]

9. In the mid-1960s, Nobel Laureate Albert Szent Gyorgi, the same man who discovered Vitamin C, isolated a substance called **3-methyl glyoxal** from urine. This substance has been shown to destroy cancer cells. The National Academy of Sciences was purportedly researching the use of this chemical.[10]

10. Dr. S. Burzynski isolated a peptide fraction called **antineoplaston** from human urine which has been found to selectively inhibit the growth of cancerous cells without significantly affecting the growth of regular cells![11]

11. In 1965 Dr. Edam from Germany recommended that Urine-Therapy as the most effective treatment for morning sickness in pregnancy and recommended that the larger teaching hospitals try this method instead of using many drugs. No side effects were ever noted, and he hoped that more doctors would look into this therapy.[12,32]

12. It has recently been discovered that fetuses (in-utero babies) use their amniotic fluid to develop their lungs. The fetus literally "breathes" this fluid into its lungs. Without this fluid, the lungs do not develop. The main component of the fluid is fetal urine.[13]

13. It has been found that in-utero surgery will not leave a scar.[14] The amniotic fluid (mostly urine) in which the fetus is contained will perfectly heal any wound in utero.

14. Today a fertility hormone called **pergonal** is made from the urine of Italian nuns.[15]

15. More scientific papers have probably been published on **urea** than on any other organic compound in the universe.

16. The longer urine stays out, the more alkaline it becomes as the urea breaks down to ammonia, leaving calcium salts to precipitate out. This is what makes old urine look so cloudy.

17. For external applications, urine's detergent properties are greatly enhanced when it is allowed to undergo bacterial fermentation. The effect of urea is stronger after having been warmed up.[16]

18. In conjunction with urea, nature's perfect denaturer, complex polymers are transformed or broken down into monomers which can then be tolerated by the body.[17]

19. **Factor S** is a hormone found in human urine which safely and naturally induces sleep.[18]

20. The high saline nature of urine acts as a good surfactant (cleaning compound) in the body, clearing old mucus which has become encrusted on the mucus membranes of the body.

21. Recycling all of one's urine, without additional fluid intake, will produce within a short time a copious amount of clear,

palatable urine. The overall purpose of this is to wash out the kidneys and purify the bloodstream. The bowel takes over the role of excreting the body's by-products.

22. Taking drugs and urine at the same time could build up dangerous levels of drugs in the body.

23. Spraying vegetable and fruit gardens with urine and water will yield fungus-free and bug-free plants, vegetables and fruit![19]

24. Urine (urea) is such a great source of nitrogen that is it now added in large quantities to farm animal feed![20]

25. Human urine has **antituberculostatic**[21], **antiprotozoal**[22], **antibacterial**[23], **antiviral**[24,25] and **antifungal**[26] properties.

26. Prostatic fluid or semen may contribute to the antibacterial activity in urine.[27]

27. Mankind could learn a lot from observing animals that haven't lost touch with their natural instincts...animals lick their wounds and infections, ingesting the "toxic" products of tissue changes and creating an immune reaction in the healthy tissues. In 1911 it was shown that by placing crude pus from a septic wound on the tongue, it would tend to cure the infection in the quickest and best manner possible.[28]

28. By recycling urine, the **protein globulins** containing specific antibodies to allergens bring about immunity from antigen-antibody conflict. These proteoses along with urea denature and digest the antigen receptors so that their biological activity is destroyed.[29]

29. **Interleukin-1** signals the hypothalamus to produce fever. Urine from febrile patients has been observed to contain a potent inhibitor of interleukin-1 induced thymocyte proliferation.[30]

30. The U.S. company, "Enzymes of America," has designed a special filter that collects the proteins from men's urinals in the 10,000 portable outhouses owned by its subsidiary firm, Porta-John. Urine contains minute amounts of proteins made by the body, including medically important ones

such as growth hormones and insulin. There is a $500 million-a-year market for these kinds of chemicals, which are usually manufactured by complicated and expensive methods such as cloning cells. The company plans to market its first major product, **Urokinase**, an enzyme that dissolves blood clots and is used to treat victims of heart attacks. The company has contracts to supply the enzymes to Sandoz, Merrell Dow and other major pharmaceutical companies.[31]

WHAT IS URINE?

Before we discuss the make-up of urine, it is important to emphasize the big picture first. It would be easy to simply account for all the substances contained in urine, and we will go through some of them later. But healing, like life in general, is not quite so simple. It consists of something that is usually overlooked in our scientific-oriented society.

Take a beautiful rose, for example. One can see the artistic shape, the radiant color, the strong, majestic appearance, and even smell the fresh and joyful perfume around it. The reason why this rose is so beautiful is because it is alive. This rose contains a life force. Without it, this same rose would be nothing more than different molecules put together, just lifeless leaves and petals. We probably would not see this radiant color, this artistic shape and strong appearance. Neither would there be any joyful fragrance. The difference is called *life*. Everything we see around us is full of life: people, animals, plants, and even minerals. Urine also contains life. It is a liquid full of energy, full of life.

Nature knows how to take care of herself. We all could learn a lot from her. In order for her to stay balanced, she uses an economically and ecologically perfect system. It is called recycling. There is no such thing as waste. Take as example the leaves which fall down to the ground during autumn. They will decompose and leach into the soil. During the next growing season the tree above will nourish itself from those substances.

6

It has been found that trees whose leaves are left on the ground will yield a bigger and better crop the next season. Another example is the water cycle. The same water is evaporated over and over again by the sun, forming clouds. After some time the water within the cloud is released, usually in the form of rain or snow. Back on the ground it will cleanse Mother Earth until it collects within a body of water, ready to be evaporated again.

This same kind of cycle also exists within ourselves. Our blood has its own cycle. The heart is pumping it through our body. The major function of the blood is to bring oxygen and nutrients to every single cell of the body. As it travels through the body, it passes through the liver and the kidneys. Let me explain the major functions of these two organs.

One of the liver's major functions is to detoxify the blood. The liver takes all the toxins out of the blood and either stores them or excretes them into the gallbladder. From the latter the toxins are excreted into the intestine in the form of bile and from there, leave the body in the form of feces. After the blood is detoxified in the liver, it flows into the kidneys (this is a simplified model).

The kidney's major function is to balance all the elements in your blood. It takes all excess amounts of vital substances out of the blood as well as excess amounts of water. This water and vital substances then form urine. Let me give you an example. The body only absorbs a given amount of vitamin C at one time. All of the excess and, therefore, unusable amounts of vitamin C within the bloodstream are using up a lot of energy. The body in its infinite wisdom eliminates all this excess amount of vitamin C through the kidneys.

Let's take a look at another example. In order for an enzyme to be activated, it needs a co-enzyme. Usually a co-enzyme is a mineral or vitamin and has to be supplied through the diet. This co-enzyme will activate and transport the enzymes into the proper place within the body. Even though our bodies may be producing more than enough enzymes, unless we are eating a diet full of nutrients, our bodies cannot function properly. To conserve energies and balance the blood, the unused enzymes also will be eliminated through the kidneys. The same story is

7

true for hormones, minerals and any other substances.

As you can see, urine is filled with vital elements. It is not waste.

Once again, the liver detoxifies the blood and excretes the toxins into the colon. The kidneys, as shown before, balance the blood's vital substances and water level.

In short, urine is simply filtered blood. It contains, in its fresh condition, only those chemicals and compounds of the blood in circulation in each of us.[33]

The Free and Free study listed approximately 200 constituents of normal urine, but stated emphatically that this was only a list of compounds of interest. They said, "It is now recognized that the urine contains thousands of compounds, and as new, more sensitive analytical tools evolve, it is quite certain that new constituents of urine will be recognized."[34]

Urine basically consists of 95% water and 5% substances including vitamins, minerals, proteins, enzymes, hormones, antibodies and amino acids. Here are some of the better known substances and their effects:

Uric acid - helps to control the process of free radical scavengers (cancer-causing molecules) in the body, controls the aging process[35] and even has a tuberculostatic effect.[36]

Antineoplaston - selectively inhibits the growth of cancerous cells without significantly affecting the growth of regular cells.[39]

H-11 - inhibits the growth of cancer cells and decreases already existing cancerous tumors, without interfering with the repair process.[38,39]

Beta-indol-acetic acid - inhibitor of somatic growth and of carcinoma and sarcoma in animals.[40]

Directin - aligns cancer cells in straight rows, end to end.[41]

3-methyl glyoxal - isolated from urine by Nobel Laureate Albert Szent Gyorgi, it is said to be able to destroy cancer cells.[42]

Allantoin - a nitrogenous crystalline substance which promotes wound healing. It is the oxidation product of uric acid.

Agglutinins and Precipitins - neutralizing activities against polio and other viruses.[43,44,45]

Gastric secretory depressants - combat the growth of peptic ulcers.[46]

Natural cortisone - a well-known and potent healing agent. Also helps the body cope with stress.[47]

Urine peptide (or polypeptide) - shows tuberculostatic activity which has been isolated in chemically pure form. Its molecular weight is said to be less than 2,000 (extremely low).[48,49]

DHEA (dehydroepiandrosterone or dehydroisoandrosterone) - is a steroid secreted by the adrenal gland and excreted in large amounts in urine. The component prevents obesity, extends the lifespan of animals, and is a possible treatment for aplastic anemia, diabetes, and breast cancer in women. DHEA stimulates the bone marrow and increases production of all bone-marrow elements including red cells, platelets, monocytes, macrophages, and lymphocytes.[50] Lower levels of DHEA seem to be related to the aging process.[51]

Protein globulins - contain antibodies to specific allergens, found to be identical to the proteins in serum (blood) immunoglobulins.[52,53]

Urea - renders the antibacterial property[54] to urine. It is an oxidizing substance which keeps the decomposing proteins dissolving in the area around the wound or infection. Because of urea, decaying or necrotic matter or tissue cannot feed off the putrefaction.[55,56,57] Urea, an end product of protein metabolism, is an organic solvent, dissolving fats and other natural body secretions. Due to its antibacterial nature, urine has a strong inhibitory effect on the growth of tubercle bacilli. NOTE: Bacteriostatic and bactericidal effects of urine increase with decreasing pH. Ingesting large quantities of ascorbic acid (Vitamin C) greatly enhances the tuberculostatic activity of urine.[58,59]

Prostoglandins - used for abortions and contraception. Can act as a birth control agent[60] as well as lowering blood pressure.[61]

Renin - maintains the body's vascular tone and thereby influences the blood pressure.[62]

Urokinase - This enzyme is a powerful artery dilating agent, resembling nitroglycerin in its ability to increase the coronary blood flow to the cardiac muscle.[63,64,65]

Interleukin-1 - activity affect both enhancer (helper)[66] and suppressor substances.[67]

Antigen-specific and **antigen-independent substances**[68]

Growth and maturation factors, including **colony-stimulating factors (CSF)** - epidermal growth factor and transforming growth factor.[69]

Factor S - safely and naturally induces sleep.[70]

Proteoses - immunologically active products of the allergic reaction.[71]

No Name Hormone - regulates the diencephalon (part of the brain) and balances the body weight.

Dr. John Herman, a New York urologist, states that the listed constituents of human urine can be carefully checked, and no items that are not found in the human diet are found in it. Percentages, of course, differ. Furthermore, he states that all urinary constituents are valuable to human metabolism in one way or another.[72]

One of the most abundant steroid hormone in our bodies is DHEA, secreted by the adrenal glands and then converted into many customized hormones to be used almost everywhere - the testes and ovaries, placenta, fetus, lungs, skin and brain. DHEA was discovered in urine in 1934. At the time, researchers could identify no purpose for it.

In the 1970's, a dramatic hormonal tune-up was on the way at the Milwaukee and North Chicago Veterans Administration Medical Centers. Endocrinologists gave human growth hormone to 28 men ages 60 to 80 in whom it was deficient.

The drug reversed the aging of their bodies by 20 years.

When the hormone was withdrawn after a year as part of the experiment, the men began to age, indicating that the growth hormone had temporarily awakened sleeping genes that had kept their bodies young.

DHEA levels in men and women decline steadily with age. Reaching a peak from ages 25 to 30, the hormone declines progressively thereafter, so that an 80-year-old person produces only 5 percent of the DHEA of a young person.

Slowly we find explanations why urine is considered the Fountain of Youth, the panacea to stay vibrant, healthy and young into old age. There are many people who prove that getting older means getting wiser and getting a chance to enjoy more of life. Former Prime Minister of India, Morarji Desai, is one of the more prominent promoter of Urine-Therapy. When we visited him in Bombay, he was 94 years old, yet his mind was sharp and quick.

Tests have shown that DHEA also inhibits breast cancer in female mice and reduces lung tumors. Applying DHEA directly to skin reduces skin cancers - papillomas and carcinomas. Lacing the animal's food with DHEA results in significant reductions of all stages of colon cancer.

Based on the stunning animal results, researchers are now giving the hormone to patients to see if it can thwart cancer, Alzheimer's disease, multiple sclerosis and other major disorders, as well as memory loss in the elderly.

HOW DOES IT WORK?

Through the years, Urine-Therapy has proven itself over and over again. As shown before, urine contains a vast amount of vital substances. Despite the research done by the scientific and medical establishment (we have over 800 specific articles on file), the mystery of how it works still remains. However, there are several hypotheses regarding the mode of action. We have to keep in mind that our science is still in an early stage and very limited in its understanding of the complicated functions of our bodies. Sure, we have come a long way. But please remember, we only know of relatively few substances contained in urine.

To accept Urine-Therapy as an effective healing method, the scientific community tries to understand how it works. However, discovering the mode of action and randomized, double-blind and crossover studies are not the only way to determine the efficacy of a given treatment. The highest placebo effect number is 30%. If the treatment shows a much higher percentage of improvement, at least the benefit of the doubt should be given.

The use of autogenous Urine-Therapy is only an extension of the methods of Jenner and Pasteur.[73] The natural defenses of the human body include an attempt to throw off the antigen-produced substances developed during the course of the disease. It is for this reason that these substances of the disease are found in the discharges. When they escape into healthy tissues, the power of the serum is raised, the activity of the leukocytes is increased, and the patient tends to recover. This is called auto-inoculation, and it is nature's method of curing a disease.[74]

Drs. Remington, Merler, and Uhr have shown that a specific fraction of a urinary protein has the ability, through binding, to inactivate a specific pathogen.[75]

In the early 1900s, Dr. Charles Duncan conducted extensive research in autogenous therapies. Urine-Therapy was one of them. He showed how every patient suffering gonorrheal urethritis carried the cure for it with him in the discharge. Autotherapy consists of arousing the natural forces within the body, by placing the crude autogenous discharge of the disease on the patient's tongue. This method of treating gonorrhea had a strong curative tendency in any stage of the disease. If given early enough, it could abort gonorrhea.[76]

The advantage of autotherapy practiced in many different forms is that it employs all of the fresh autogenous unchanged tissue toxins from the causative and complicating micro-organisms. It employs all, and the exact substances nature employs when a natural cure is made. The patient is carrying with him his own cure in the very form adapted by nature to cure his condition. There being no foreign proteins present, anaphylaxis (shock) never follows in the administration of endogenous fluid.[77]

Guinea pigs sensitized to ovalbumin excrete the antigen in their urine in a therapeutic concentration which prevents anaphylactic death after injection of a challenge dose of the ovalbumin.[78]

Tourvill, Bienenstock and Tomasi demonstrated gA-antibodies in normal urine against E. Coli. In immunized individuals gA-urinary antibodies have been demonstrated against S. typhi[79], polio virus[80], and tetanus toxoid. In addition, a gA-rheumatoid factor has been isolated from the urine of patients with high serum titers of rheumatoid factor.[82] These antibodies and factors will help the immune system to fight the disease. Clinical observations show that the more urine is concentrated and the more receptors are produced (by exposure to antigens prior to injection or ingestion), the better the results. Furthermore, they show that there seems to be an enhancement or stimulation of the immune system, mostly of the T-cell population. In several patients exhibiting a low T-cell count, the T-cell population was restored to normal after finishing treatments of immuno-tolerance (Urine-Therapy).[83]

Because of the above-mentioned receptors, Urine-Therapy is capable of controlling a wide range of food, extrinsic and chemical sensitivities.[84] Sublingual administration of the correct dose of urine from allergic patients provides therapeutic control of their allergic symptoms.[85]

As of today, the pharmaceutical industry has performed the most scientific research on Urine-Therapy. Their idea is to find the specific substance responsible for a cure and produce it artificially. Their only interest in this research is a chance to discover a profitable, saleable product. Their intention is to make money. That is why they are in business.

I do not believe that this single substance will ever be found. Every second, thousands of different substance interact with each other. Each and every one of them has to be in proper balance. Only urine used as a whole product will give the body the necessary healing receptors and elements.

Let the body's infinite wisdom take care of itself and support it by recycling the Water of Life along with a very healthy, nutritious diet.

HOW IS URINE-THERAPY DONE?

Several attempts have been made to elevate treatments with urine to scientific levels. With the invention of the hypodermic needle and syringe, urine was injected. This began in Europe, but as far back as 1863, it was mentioned in *The Physiological Memoirs of Surgeon-General Hammond, U.S. Army.*[86]

Today there are very few physicians who are using urine injections in their practice. The reasons are many.

Fortunately, Urine-Therapy is very simple in its application. For thousands of years people healed themselves of a myriad of diseases without the blessing of modern medicine. The survival of mankind never was and never will be dependent on our "high- tech medicine." The reason why we have made it up to today is because of the body's innate wisdom to fight disease. The biggest improvements we have experienced to lengthen our lifespan and improve our health are sanitation, refrigeration, and central heating.

Before we elaborate on the practical application, first a word of **CAUTION!** *Urine-Therapy and prescriptions, over the counter or recreational drugs do not mix.* This combinations can be dangerous to your health!

Urine-Therapy consists of two basic parts: the internal application and the external application. Both parts complement each other and are necessary for best results. There are many different ways of using urine. After the initial experience one will find his or her own personal way of application. Because urine is produced to one's needs, only your own urine should be taken for internal use.

Here are the different ways of application:

INTERNAL APPLICATION

Only **fresh** and your **own** urine should be used.

1. **Drinking.** The mid-stream of the first morning urine is taken. Begin with 2-3 oz. and increase it to your personal, comfortable level.

2. **Fasts.** Fasts with urine and water are practiced for one or more days. J.W. Armstrong, a renowned urine therapist from England, let his patients fast for up to 45 days. *Fasts are only recommended under trained, medical supervision.*

3. **Implants.** Take an ear syringe containing 2-3 oz. of urine. The urine is kept in the colon as long as possible. Helps to detoxify the liver through the portal vein.

4. **Enemas.** Use either only urine or add a tea such as Camomile or other herbal fluids.

5. **Gargle.** Urine is kept in the mouth 20-30 minutes, or as long as possible, for gum problems and other lesions of the mouth and tongue.

6. **Douche.** For any vaginal discomfort or cleansing, a solution of Golden Seal and urine will provide comfort and healing.

7. **Eye and ear drops.** Any pain, burning and tiredness in the eyes may get relief with a few urine drops placed into the eyes. The ears also benefit greatly if receiving a few urine drops for ear pain and discomfort.

8. **Urine sniffing.** This is the most effective way of treatment for any sinus congestion and upper respiratory problems.

9. **Homeopathic tincture.** A 1/1,000,000 solution of urine is prepared. This is taken under the tongue. Start with 2 drops and increase it up to 10 drops a day. This homeopathic tincture is very easy to prepare.

a. Obtain and clean a medicine dropper and six small tubes (available in drug stores).
b. Place 18 drops of water into each tube and place them into a cup to avoid spillage.
c. Collect a mid-stream urine specimen and place 2 drops into tube #1.
d. Succuss the tube 25-50 times. To do this, clench the tube in a closed hand with the thumb over the tube mouth. Sharply pound the fist into the other palm. This is succussion and is very important.
e. Then place 2 drops from tube #1 into tube #2. Repeat the succussion process. Rinse the dropper after each use. Continue the dilution-succussion processes until all six tubes have been used.
f. The mixture in tube #6 represents a 6x or 1/1,000,000 dilution.

EXTERNAL APPLICATION

Urine for external use is preferred to be **several days old** and **warmed up**.

1. **Rubbings**. Urine is massaged into the body. Rubbings usually are done for any kind of skin lesions from a simple rash to eczema and cancer. The rubbing may last from 20 minutes to 1 hour in duration.
2. **Foot baths**. Very effective for athlete's foot or any skin problem on the feet.
3. **Urine packs**. Take a piece of cloth or a cotton ball, depending on the applicable size, and soak it in urine. Then attach it to the treated area.

BABIES

Urine from the baby's diaper is preferred for rubbing and a homeopathic tincture for internal use. If urine is not available in a sufficient amount, the mother's urine may be used.

OLDER CHILDREN

Urine enemas are most often used for children. During the 1940s, German doctors applied urine enemas to children with measles, chicken pox and whooping cough. They found that if urine enemas were given during the incubation period, the children exhibited only a mild form of the disease, if any at all.[87]

For those of you who desire a **beautiful skin** and a **healthy complexion**, massage fresh urine into your skin daily in the morning or the evening. This is the secret of many famous sex symbols and beauty queens.

IMPORTANT: Urine-Therapy, like any other natural healing therapy, will generate a **healing crisis**. What is this healing crisis? After taking urine for some time (1 day, 1 week, or 1 month, depending on your body), the body starts to detoxify. During that period, all the stored toxins and diseases - and this may go back to the earliest childhood disease - will be released by the body. There are only a few ways to throw out these toxins, either through the skin, colon, breath or mouth. The body may also take care of certain viruses by raising the temperature and producing a fever. What it comes down to is that during a healing crisis one may have symptoms like rashes, sweating, fever, boils, diarrhea, vomiting, headache and coughing. Usually they only last for a few hours to a few days. After the crisis, one feels better and a step healthier. It is strongly recommended not to stop the Urine-Therapy during that natural process.

The morning urine is the richest and best urine to drink. This is partially due to the greater level of hormonal secretion that takes place in the late night hours when the body is totally relaxed and repairing itself.

The practice of Urine-Therapy is not dose-sensitive Obviously the amount of urine one consumes will have a direct relationship to the voracity of any healing crisis (i.e. detoxification) that one might experience, and the speed of recovery.

Starting with one ounce a day and working up to 6 or 8

ounces is a very comfortable way to slowly introduce the body, mind, and spirit to this beautiful therapy.

Often I am asked how to overcome the conditioned disgust. There are several methods. I will explain them a little later. First, I would like to give you some other thoughts.

Over most of the civilized world, blood and blood derivatives are used medicinally with no thought of the distaste usually associated with Urine-Therapy. We utilize packed cells, plasma, white cells, and various other fractions of the blood without pause. Urine, too, is only a derivative of the blood. We see babies nursing from their mother's nipple and we are not disgusted. We drink cow's milk with no hesitation, and we eat cheeses from cows, goats, and other animals. We even go so far as to spoil these milks and drink them as yoghurt, sour cream and buttermilk with no antagonism from our neighbors or friends! Beyond that, we eat raw meat and blood wurst, and we consider a delight kidneys from young animals. Yet we could not consider eating or drinking the urine from these same sources. As we have seen before, urine contains, in its fresh condition, only those chemicals and compounds of the blood in circulation in each of us. If it is not toxic or disgusting while in the blood, why does it suddenly become so abhorrent in the urine?

If it is not the color (and it is not, since we consume large quantities of wine in the same shades), and it is not the smell (and it is not, since we consume large amounts of cheeses with more horrendous odors), and it is not the temperature (and it is not), then maybe it is the taste. How many people do you know who have drunk enough urine to be sure of its taste? I do know quite a few. Those who do regularly consume their own urine say that the taste is mild and not disturbing, and that it is salty like ocean water.

Now, a good way to undo conditioned behavior with regard to perception of urine is to rinse, gargle and swish with fresh urine. The flavor, consistency, and feeling of the experience will become familiar after a while, and the disgust to your own rich bodily fluids will be a thing of the past.

Rubbing urine into the body (fresh or stale) is also a wonderful way to become accustomed to your living water.

If the idea of drinking one's own water is still a problem, pour a few ounces into the morning juice. This solution should be drunk as soon as possible, for urine breaks down very rapidly. Try to graduate from drinking the dilution to taking it straight. Some people prefer to take it straight, followed by a "chaser" of pure water or some other healthy liquid.

Saying "thank you" to your body just before drinking urine will help you to realize the value of this golden liquid. Your body produced it for you. Celebrate life and put the urine into a beautiful wine glass. After all, it is the most valuable water on earth.

WHAT'S NUTRITION GOT TO DO WITH IT?

Anything that surrounds you, anything you eat and breathe, and anything you massage or inject into your body will affect you one way or another. It either improves your health or it depresses your health, including the immune system.

When was the last time you thought about the purpose of eating? Often one enjoys a meal with family and friends during social interactions, attends a business meeting during mealtimes, or just grabs something to eat - anything - to satisfy hunger.

How often do we ask questions like "where does the food come from?", "how was it produced?", "how does it affect my body?" and "what should I eat?"

These are vital questions. I will answer only some of them in this booklet. The book *The Miracles of Urine-Therapy* discusses nutrition and a healthy lifestyle in more depth.

The major purpose of food consumption is to provide the body with the essential nutrients needed for growth, repair and maintenance. These nutrients are proteins, carbohydrates, fats, minerals, vitamins, enzymes and trace elements.

Making a long story short, the big question is: Do we get enough of the essential nutrients in our diet? The answer is definitely - NO!

Dr. Michael Colgan, founder of the Colgan Institute of Nutritional Science, calls it a problem of depleted foods. He says, "Americans are malnourished, even when we succeed at eating a balanced diet. Our systems still suffer from the actual lack of nutrients in foods. Produce and natural foods, such as whole grains, are robbed of their nutritional potential from exhausted soil and artificial fertilizers. Wheat from the U.S. has been rejected at China's ports because the protein content was so low. U.S. Agriculture Department figures show that today's wheat often contains only 20% of the protein it used to have!"

It is a fact that our soil is depleted of minerals and important trace elements. Furthermore, pesticides have killed the necessary bacteria and insects in the soil to produce natural nitrogen. Weakened and unhealthy plants growing in such soil are inclined to get diseases or be eaten by insects. (Remember, healthy plants are less likely to have those problems.) Therefore more pesticides and fungicides are sprayed to keep these weak plants alive. And the vicious cycle goes on.

Our meat production is no better off. Forty percent of all the antibiotics are sold to farmers. If you are a meat eater or a milk drinker, you will consume traces of these antibiotics in your meals - not once, not twice but every time you consume meat or dairy products. These traces of antibiotics, which pile up in your body, kill the healthy bacteria in your system. It is no surprise to see this epidemic of yeast infections. Yeast, though necessary in the body, will grow out of control in the absence of healthy bacteria.

This brings us back to the basics. Whatever you eat will affect your body and in turn will affect your urine. The better your diet is, the better your urine will taste. Unless you provide the body with the essential nutrients, it does not have the raw material to keep up good health. Urine contains many of the essential nutrients, and by drinking it, they will be recycled. Nevertheless, if the body does not get certain nutrients replenished through the diet, eventually they will be depleted. What may follow are chronic degenerative diseases of all kinds.

How can we avoid this? Where can we get these essential nutrients?

There one pecial food products which I highly recommend. The first product is one of the simplest life forms on earth, but without it, we probably would not exist. It produces 80% of all the oxygen on earth. Its name is Aphanizomenon-flos-aquae. This is a blue-green algae. This algae grows naturally in a clean lake fed by mineral-rich rivers from volcanic mountains.

Algae are highly efficient photosynthesizers, more so than green plants. They utilize light energy, carbon dioxide from the air, and hydrogen and oxygen from the water to synthesize a high-energy form of protein, carbohydrates (starches and sugars), lipids (fats), nucleic acids (DNA and RNA), vitamins, co-factors, chlorophylls and pigments. Because algae contains as high as 60% consumable protein, it can be substituted for meat. It is very helpful in increasing the assimilation and utilization of proteins when on a vegetarian, macrobiotic, and/or strictly raw food diet.

Protein is especially important for any woman who is pregnant or nursing. This algae will provide a terrific alternative to high consumption of meat and dairy products.

Healthy, nutrient-rich food will keep your body strong. The article "Drug of the Sea," in *Discover Magazine*, May 1988, shows just this principle in the following statement. "An algae extract stimulates animals immune systems by 225 percent and cells in cultures by 2,000 percent."

IMPORTANT: Algae is not a drug. It is an unprocessed and unaltered food. It does not make any medical claims. Algae simply provides the body with the so important essential nutrients. *For further information on this algae, please see last page of this booklet.*

Finally, let's look at a healthy diet. We all have our own special way of eating to feel great. In general, food should be organically grown and of high quality. A healthy diet contains fresh vegetables, fresh fruit, whole grains, seeds, nuts, beans, algae, natural sweeteners such as honey, and sometimes a limited intake of dairy products. Also for some people meat intake is acceptable.

Not recommended is anything made of white flour, white rice, and white sugar. Avoid anything processed, irradiated, artificially colored and/or flavored. Avoid anything that was sprayed with herbicides, pesticides or fungicides. If you are still a red meat eater, try to replace it with fowl free of antibiotics and hormones, fish, or best of all - try the algae.

It is not an easy task to change to a wholesome diet. Decreasing the intake of not-recommended foods and increasing the intake of recommended foods is a good way to start this process. But remember, any change requires time. It takes several generations to adopt to a new way of life - a new diet. Any radical change may be unhealthy for your system. Your body needs time to adopt to the a new diet. If you have been eating meat all your life and so have your forefathers, please take your time. Listen to your body and follow what feel right. Enjoy your meals!

There is one more important part I would like to cover - the skin. The skin is the largest organ. It works as a detoxifier, regulates the water and mineral balance, and protects the body. It is the first line of defense. The skin also absorbs anything we massage in, bath in or put onto it.

Urine has great rejuvenation properties and we have seen many great benefits with applying it to the skin. However, it does not protect the skin from irritants commonly used in everyday life.

In our industrial age we are dealing with harsh chemicals, dyes, fuels, lubricants, paints, water and air pollutants, cleaning material, oils, bleaches, chlorine, alcohol, grease, oils and acetone inside and outside the home.

We strongly recommend to protect the skin from absorbing all these different chemicals. Many of them are quite toxic to our body.

It is not an easy task to protect ourselves from the ever growing chemical exposure in our food supply, our air and our water. The sharp increase in allergies and immune deficiency diseases is a warning that it is time to make changes in our environment and our lifestyles. I urge you to take steps in your own life to implement changes which will benefit every living creature as well as Mother Earth. Together, we can build a heatlher future for our children.

ANY CASE HISTORIES?

This booklet is not intended to give many case histories. There are literally hundreds of experiences listed in other books on Urine-Therapy. For others, please refer to the included booklist.

Dr. V.P.M.:

I am a qualified and experienced medical doctor with the highest degrees both in medicine and surgery. On March 12, 1986, I was diagnosed with cancer of the ary-epiglottic area (throat) with enlarged cervical lymph nodes. After receiving chemotherapy and a course of cobalt therapy I was to be operated on. Between August and October I tried Urine-Therapy. By October 5, 1986, my disease was totally cured and the proposed surgery was cancelled.

I have not only recovered in a medical sense, but I am also leading a fully active professional life. In other words, even the quality of my life has improved. I feel the same zeal which I had 30 years ago.

Mr. Q., New York:

I was laughing and snickering in the back of the room. After all, who would take anyone seriously talking about drinking one's own urine to heal any disease! My main concern at the time was how I was going to handle this diagnosis of full-blown AIDS and with what "spirituality" was I going to handle an oral, palatal Kaposi's sarcoma lesion that was supposed to spread relentlessly throughout my body. I was told just two months prior that the prognosis could be about two years, more if fortunate, and to seriously consider preparing a "living will."

For obvious reasons, I seemed to be much more tolerant to the idea of applying urine topically for all sorts of conditions. My right foot was the epitome of necrosis. For months doctors had prescribed many different medicated creams for a vicious case of athlete's foot/ringworm. Nothing seemed to work. After all, the root of the problem was the immune system's not functioning at full capacity. I couldn't wait to go home to put my own urine on the foot.

That evening was the first time in many months that the tingling itch did not drive me into a frenzy! I actually got a full night of sleep. Not only did the ringworm condition totally disappear after a few weeks, but the dry, cracked and painful skin all around my toes and bottom of the foot had totally changed in color and texture! New skin had grown in and was soft as a baby's. It had a beautiful new flushed, almost orange-like color and it just did not appear to be my own skin!

I anxiously began to research the field of autogenous fluids and, shortly thereafter, decided that recycling my urine was really a harmless form of auto-toleration based on theories not much different than those in the science of homeopathy.

Drinking my urine was not that difficult, but deconditioning myself was the real chore. I felt betrayed by society upon learning that our urine is not a poisonous, toxic and filthy substance that our bodies so heroically expel. Since urine is filtered and cleansed blood, and the blood is 95% water, how many dangerous substances can there really be in urine?

Starting with just a small ounce, I gradually began drinking my body's own distilled preparation with respect instead of disgust. I then graduated to drinking up to 8 ounces daily.

Over the next seven months the Kaposi's sarcoma lesion became increasingly smaller until it disappeared totally! The mouth ulcers that used to plague me, stinging during meals, have not returned even once. I used to have monthly outbreaks of genital herpes, but I am elated to say that autogenous Urine-Therapy has produced a state of tolerance even against the herpes virus that sooner or later, in conjunction with Ebstein-Barr virus (EBV), Cytomegalovirus (CMV), and Papilloma virus would have surely complicated my existence and further weakened my immune system...just a matter of time. I have **NEVER** felt better in my life. Now, I no longer fear for my life.

Mr. B., Georgia:

I am a PWA (person with AIDS). I have been doing Urine-Therapy for three months. My fatigue and dizziness dissipated within the first month. I experienced intense eye itchiness. A few drops of fresh urine stopped it immediately. If I forget to take the urine one day, the next day I will pay for it with fatigue. Also my lymph gland swelling is reduced by 50%.

Mr. L., New York:

I have been doing Urine-Therapy for four months now. I am a PWA. My only symptom was a low T-cell count. My last test showed my T-cell count went up from 285 to 489.

Mrs. B., Florida:

I had been suffering from migraine headaches for 35 years. In addition, rheumatoid arthritis had plagued me for the last 15 years. The pain and swelling in the joints of my hands was unbelievable. I could not leave the house without painkillers. For four months, half of my foot was covered with a fungus. I tried many different treatments. Unfortunately, it only got worse. At 198 pounds, I was overweight as well. Needless to say, I was not the picture of health. Then a friend told me about Urine-Therapy. I soaked my feet in urine, and within a week, the fungus cleared up. Then I started drinking my own urine. The result was just incredible. Four and a half months later, my weight was down to 130 pounds. I have lost 68 pounds! My arthritis is gone, and my headaches are gone. I feel like I am 20 years old again. Thank you for telling me about Urine-Therapy.

Mr. D., Georgia:

I am a PWA. Three months prior to starting Urine-Therapy I experienced heavy night sweats, and I needed 18 hours of sleep daily! Also my skin was very dry and ashy looking. All these symptoms got resolved within 10 days of Urine-Therapy. I now play one hour of basketball every day. What a difference!

Mr. T., California:

Seven years ago, I was diagnosed with a lymphatic disorder. The doctors first thought it was Hodgkin's disease. During a vacation in Brazil I contracted some parasites. One was Shigella and the other was Giardia. I was treated with penicillin and many other antibiotics. But I still lost weight, and the diarrhea was persistent. Then the new testing for AIDS came out, and I tested positive. I had constant problems with thrush. I also suffered from Kaposi's sarcoma intermittently over portions of my body. My energy level was very low.

To make a long story short, I started Urine-Therapy. The first treatment with urine was on my skin. The second day I noticed that the KS lesions were starting to fade. Then I started to drink my own urine. I took about one ounce a day at the beginning. My thrush went away. Every time when I apply urine to any aberration or sore on my skin, it all but disappears. The KS lesion I was talking about is not even one-fourth the original size. Also my energy level is much higher. I had colitis. I no longer have an inflamed colon. I am steady as a clock and do not suffer anymore from chronic diarrhea. So evidently this is working for me.

Mr. M., New York:

I am a PWA. My major problem was parasites. My stool sample contained pus, large amounts of yeast and several parasites. My last test came back totally clear. No more pus and no more parasites!

Mr. A., Georgia:

I am a PWA and have been doing Urine-Therapy for two and one-half months. My Lymphadenopathy was gone within 48 hours after starting the urine. I had a severe acne problem on my back. After five weeks the skin is clear. My energy level increased enormously within a few days of drinking my urine.

Mr. S., New York:

One and one-half months ago I was diagnosed with gonorrhea, anal sores and herpes. I took medication and the condition improved. But two weeks later the herpes came back even worse. So I started Urine-Therapy. Within two or three days, everything cleared up totally. What was even more amazing to me is the parasite problem I suffered for quite some time got resolved inadvertently with Urine-Therapy, while treating my herpes.

Mr. G.K.T.:

The last 40 years I have suffered from eczema, and the last 20 years from amoebic dysentery. My physicians had assured me that I will suffer like this for the rest of my life. To my utter surprise, I got rid of both diseases by this wonderful remedy, Urine-Therapy. You will be further surprised to know that there were some side effects too; but not of the usual nature, which you suffer in allopathic treatments. I also suffered from falling hair and dandruff. I always used to have cracks in my feet and even on my lips during all the seasons. Once every few months I also suffered from stomatitis. I got rid of all the above complaints and ailments unknowingly, as a side effect of this therapy.

My wife was a regular patient for more than 20 years and was suffering from numerous diseases like ear trouble, vertigo, constipation, pain in the joints and many more. She tried the best available treatments in allopathy, homeopathy and ayurvedic medicine but without any results. At last she tried Urine-Therapy and got rid of all her ailments miraculously.

And if this is not enough, my younger son, 17 years old, suffered from hematuria for more than a year. The doctors thought that something was seriously wrong with his kidneys and recommended an intravenous polygraph. I persuaded my son to start drinking his urine for 30 days and then to take another urine test. After that period of time, the report of the urine test came back absolutely normal!

Mrs. B., New York:

One day I wanted to make sure my iron was turned off before I left the house. So I checked the iron surface with the palm of my hand, expecting it to be cold. To my surprise, the iron was very hot. Unfortunately, the damage was already done. I burned my hand with at least second degree burns. It was very painful, to say the least.

Then I remembered that some weeks earlier I had stored away a bottle containing urine. I got that old urine from the bottle and covered my burns with it. The pain soon left. A few hours later, my hand looked and felt as if nothing had happened to it. No blisters, no scars, no redness.

The effectivness of this simple but powerful liquid is amazing.

Mr. M., Florida:

If it is of interest to you for any research purposes, I nearly died from the reactions of several strong antibiotics administered over several months of lung infections. I have been hospitalized three times in the past year for the resulting gastro-intestinal problems created by the medication. After the most recent hospital stay, I refused to continue with the medication. Most of the problems began to clear up within a few days. However, my rectal bleedings from colitis and internal hemorrhoids continued.

In the meantime a friend told me that in the Tennessee Hills, where he was raised, urine enemas were used for similar problems. On July 31, 1988, I began using urine for daily enemas. By the end of the following week, the bleeding had stopped completely, and as of this date (September 25, 1988), I have not passed a single drop of blood.

Mr. P.O.H., Florida

Dear Dr. Bartnett, thank you so much for the work you are doing.

I am taking it every morning internally. Then, I go into the shower with a cup full of the water of life and massage it all over. After 10 minutes I start the shower and wash it off.

This feels so good on my skin, which is clean and soft. My gray hair is getting black again, and my constipation in gone.

I do not know what I would do without it. Fortunately there is always enough of it.

Thank you again for all you are doing.

Mr. J.P., Indianapolis

Dear Dr. Bartnett, I have read your exciting and welcome account of Urine-Therapy and started using it immediately with definite, effective results.

I had used it topically on a serious arm and hand infection last year, after reading an account, in Readers Digest (*The King Crab Story*). A crew member had cured a seriously infected leg with his own urine.

The thought of using it internally never occurred to me, and I took to it like a duck takes to water.

I am a senior citizen, and read your wonderful article in the *Health Freedom News*.

Ms. Tara, Toowoomba, Australia

In 1988, I had cancer in the bowel, liver and lymph system. For the cancer in the bowel I had three operations within three months, which left me only skin and bones. For the liver and lymph glands I was offered chemotherapy, which I declined. All the anaesthetics, antibiotics and postoperative drugs had weakened my immune system to rock bottom, and because of this I had already started to lose great bunches of hair.

I had asked God, in prayer, to bring to me anything I needed to get well again, and at this time I was given by a friend a *Water of Life* book written by J.W. Armstrong.

I thanked the Father within me, and I knew that what I had read would totally heal me if I now would apply it to my own situation and condition. I decided not to tell my doctor or anyone until I felt totally healed. I did not want any discouragement or negative influences. I kept up with my meditation and relaxation techniques.

I drank wheatgrass juice, mixed with lettuce juice to make it more palatable, and other veggie juices. I ate plenty of salads and greens, no meat, no cooked foods, no dairy products, nor oils or fats for three months, to heal my liver. I daily rubbed my whole body, including my hair and scalp, with urine. As the Bible says: "Anoint the body!" The skin is an absorbing organ for the lymph glands. I would do this in the afternoon and shower the next morning. I also drank my own "Water of Life" in between meals, early morning and during the night.

Mahatma Gandhi drank a glass of his own urine every day for prevention of illness. It sustained him during his long fasts since the urine is rich in vitamins, minerals, and enzymes. Shipwrecked people, or those in the desert have survived on it. Countless others are using it as a daily ritual, and as Armstrong mentions in his book, never have a cold or flu again.

Nine months later, I went to the doctor looking and feeling well, which was a great surprise to him. A blood test showed no remaining trace of cancer.

In 1990, on a trip to Central Australia, I met a Nursing Sister who is training nurses in a large city hospital. She told me there is a new drug in America, which is having a good success rate as a cancer cure (Editor: Anti-neoplaston developed by Dr. Burzynski). Because of its high cost, the Australian government is not importing it to be used there. She said it was made up of concentrated urine from thousands of people!

30

Several weeks later someone else told me, she too had read an article claiming that urine is being collected for this purpose in the USA from convents and monasteries! If so, why not simply take one's own, which is exactly adjusted in the antibodies needed at the time for one's own healing not someone else's antibodies from other diseases.

If people find it difficult at first to even think of drinking their own urine, they can start with a little amount diluted with pure water. Gradually increase the urine and decrease the water. Another important factor to know is not to take any medication while pricticing Urine-Therapy. Most of the times, naturopathic or homeopathic remedies do not interfere with urine therapy, but rather assist it.

If one wishes to recycle what Mother Nature has originally provided for us, half fill a bucket with water, put it into your bathroom, use for urinating, and cover it with a towel. Empty it at least daily onto your garden soil, around flowers, veggies, lemon and other trees. Mother Nature will be grateful and will reward you for it. (In drought stricken areas it saves water by not flushing the toilet.)

According to my understanding from reading J.W. Armstrong's writings, I strongly believe that the infectious eye problems of our Australian Aboriginal Children could be relieved simply and inexpensively by using Uropathy. In acute cases it is recommended to wash the eyes several times daily with fresh, still-warm urine. All that is needed is an eye-glass. I do it myself when my eyes are red or irritated form the sun, wind or dust particles.

It is my great desire, and in gratitude to the Universe of which we are all a part, to share my healing experience. Hopefully others with Cancer, AIDS or other afflictions will have the courage and enough self-love to choose Uropathy for their own healing. Then they too can come forward and share their experiences with others.

May all my brothers and sisters in God be healed in body, mind and soul.

Mr. CvDK, Netherland

Dear Dr. Bartnett, I was delighted and in a wonderful way surprised when I came across your book, *The Miracles of Urine-Therapy*, in a bookstore while visiting Los Angeles. I was looking for this book without knowing of its existence. It combines a couple of very important issues that have been on my mind and heart the last years.

I would like to tell you some more about this. My story of discovering the application of Urine-Therapy started one and a half years ago. I was visiting an ashram (of Haidakhandi Babaji) in India. There is a tradition of karma-yoga, involving a lot of physical labor, carrying stones, etc.. Well, a couple of hours into my first day of working with stones ended quickly with a hugh rock falling from four feet high onto my left foot. I was not wearing closed shoes so the stone ripped almost all the flesh and my toenail from, luckily, only the middle toe. The other ones just turned a little bit blue afterwards. I went to the improvised hospital in the ashram which is, itself, situated in a secluded place in the Himalayas. They could not repair anything and said the toe was broken (later, back in the Netherlands, it turned out that the toe had been broken at the time). They put a bandage around it with anti-septic creme on the wound. For the next days I had severe pains and the wound kept on bleeding quite a bit. I was starting to get worried. Everyone was warning me that terrible infections could happen, and I had the impression that the treatment with the anti-septic creme wasn't doing any good to the healing process.

Then I met this woman who told me that a cloth soaked in my own urine would probably do a better job. I was a little bit suspicious about this idea but very soon I felt this intuitive "yes" to trying it out. I did, and it was amazing to see how quickly my toe started to heal. A brand new pink skin appeared at the place where brfore was only an undefinable mass of red and black stuff, not at all much looking like my

32

toe. Pieces of old and damaged skin fell off and within a couple of days the whole thing looked pretty much like a normal toe again. I kept the cloth wet all the time sometimes with fresh urine when I went for a pee and sometimes with old urine which I collected in a bottle.

In the small library in the ashram I found, during this week, since I wasn't able to do any work anymore, this book of J.W. Armstrong called *The Water of Life*. I read it and I immediately felt I had come across something very important. It felt like discovering a long forgotten secret. I just knew that it was true what he was writing although at the same time it felt strange to my western-programmed mind. I felt happy that the stone on my toe had brought me to this discovery. Nowadays I have gotten used to drinking urine, and I have my share of the Water of Life almost every morning.

Now I will tell you also a little bit more how it connects with some other aspects of my life. In a way, it is your book that has confirmed some of my feelings. It added a very important new aspect about the balancing of female and male energy.

Half a year before I went to India, I finished my study with a Master in Classics. My thesis was on ancient Greek gynecology and I made a comparison with the Indian Ayurvedic healing system. When I started working on this I somehow felt that the principles from Ayurveda were very familiar to me. The aspect of female-male polarity on all kind of levels – from social constructs to yin-yang in medicine, and from mythology to my very own being and sexuality – is very important to me. So I was really surprised to read in your book about this specified connection of the Water of Life and the balancing of female and male energies.

Also Urine-Therapy seems to be connected with Shiva, and Babaji was said to be a direct incarnation of Shiva. The healing aspect of the snake plays another important role for me.

Well, I have written quite a long letter but I think you will understand why. The whole subject is close to my heart, and I feel very inspired by knowing that there are other people around working on the same things and are most probably able to teach me more about it. I really hope to hear from you soon.

G.B., Australia

It is not unusual for me to become interested in the Water of Life since I have been natural minded for the last 20 years and feel better than I did 50 years ago. When I first read about Urine-Therapy, I was as skeptical as everyone else, and after reading John Armstrong's, *The Water of Life*, still it did not make me a believer.

Prior to reading this book I was going to a doctor in prevention medicine. The doctor asked me to bring in my urine and I was to give it to his nurse who, to my knowledge, did some processing and then injected it into my arm. I was to have 10 or 15 treatments, but then I became curious and asked the doctor more questions. He said this kind of therapy has been practiced in Europe for many years. I asked for some literature, but when he failed to produce it, I stopped going to the doctor.

I live on a mini-farm where I have a few chickens, sheep and pygmy goats. Pygmy goats are not far removed from their wilderness state, brought over to the United States in approx. 1954. Mine was a beautiful healthy goat with long shiny hair and a beautiful set of horns that curved around his head. One day when I went to the barnyard to feed "Shogan," my pygmy goat, he raised his rear hind leg and with perfect aim, urinated directly into his open mouth. There was a large trough of water available for him and he could have all the drinking water he wanted. Drinking his own urine convinced me as I am a firm believer that animals have better instincts than humans.

I started to drink my own urine, in fact, gave some of it to

34

one of my German Shepherd dogs that had lost most of her hair off her back. It was soon after that her hair all grew in and her health improved. One day I received the shock of my life when I expelled a worm at least 12 inches long. I still have it preserved in alcohol. I went to the Doctor and he asked me if I had ever lived in the tropics and I stated I had, as I taught school in the Panama Canal zone in the 1930s. It was hard for me to believe that a worm could live inside me for some 50 years.

I am daily taking my own water. It just feels right.

Mr. B.N.,Michigan

Dear Dr. Bartnett, in 1984 I was afflicted with a debilitating disease. At the time I required 14-16 hours of sleep daily, medication for headache symptoms, and antidepressants for the mental depression which accompanied it. This was very difficult to manage for someone who previously was able to work 18 hours daily, play sports, and perform very well in school.

My family background included nursing a mother through terminal cancer some years before. As a family, we not only learned that cancer could be defeated with detoxification and supplementation, but also stopped all chemical use on our farm.

This helped my father's decision to stop all medical therapy and seek alternative help. Several programs were available and a program was designed for my needs. After two months work, I returned to professional school and graduated at the top of my class.

After avoiding chemicals, short-chained sugars, and other non-healthy attitudes and practices for several years, my evaluation was pretty good. It was then I heard of Urine-Therapy.

Although disgusting at first, Urine-Therapy has done the following for me:

- Eliminated belching, stomach upset, constipation and depression after eating;
- Decreased the size of several lumps on my body identified by two doctors as cysts;
- Increased my energy levels;
- Further eliminated my headaches;
- Helped me lose unnecessary weight; and
- I can eat junk food every once in a while and not get incredibly sick. If I do eat a food that makes me sick, Urine-Therapy will turn me around very quickly;

I only have one recommendation for people I speak to and that is: Do it! Get plenty of advice from doctors who work with Urine-Therapy, and plan to fast as well. It works!

Mr.M.L., New York

Words cannot describe the joy I am feeling at this moment.

Three years ago I met a wonderful lady, my wife. She was reading an old book someone gave her. She showed me the book. That was the first time I had a chance to read something about the Water of Life. I read the book very fast and decided to think about it.

It took me three months to build up enough courage and drink my own Water of Life. After a few weeks, I was feeling so good inside and out, I was convinced that this was the Fountain of Youth Cortes was looking for.

All my family and friends heard about my discovery. Most of them rejected the idea of using this therapy for most simple and fatal diseases. "I would rather die," some said. But that did not discourage me. More and more people heard my theory.

This letter was written because I finally met a person who was desperate. The doctors gave him few months to live. He wrote a testament and divided everything he owns among his family and friends. Then, he said goodbye to the ones who lived in his native land.

David had chronic diarrhea, vomited everything, had a permanent headache and a terrible pain throughout his bones. The worst feeling was knowing that he probably passed on the disease to his wife. "Martin," he said, "you have no idea of the agony I am feeling." This man was almost ready to kill himself, but he had no energy to do it. He was really desperate.

That was when his sister called me for help. She had heard my theory and decided to call me. I explained to them how the book describes the therapy. I told him to drink it with grapefruit juice at first, until he became familiar with the taste. To the surprise of everyone he did it, he drank his urine. Let me tell you after the first three days this man felt so good he could not thank me enough for saving him from all the suffering.

At the time of this letter, David had gained 25 pounds and was enjoying a second honeymoon. With tears in his eyes, he told me that he was willing to do anything to help me spread the word.

David's brother, who also has AIDS, called me to tell me that he is drinking the Water of Life. And after a few days of therapy, he also regained his appetite and is feeling terrific.

The first time I heard about the Urine-Therapy was when I was five or six years old. I am 38 now. The person from whom this theory came at the time was my great grandfather in the Dominican Republic.

BIBLIOGRAPHY

1. *Holy Bible*, King James Edition, Thomas Nelson Publisher, 1979, John 4:14.
2. Staff Reporter, "Jordan's Nine-Day War," *Newsweek*, October 5, 1970, p. 36.
3. Smith, Homer W., "De Urina," *Journal of the American Medical Association*, Vol. 155, No. 10, July 3, 1954, pp. 899-902.
4. Wallnofer, H., et al., *Chinese Folk Medicine*, Crown Publisher, N.Y.C., 1965, pp. 70-71.
5. Sathyamurthy, "Management of Chronic Leprosy Ulcers with Urine-Therapy," *Bethany Leprosy Clinic*, September, 1980, p. 2.
6. Krishnamurthy, P., "Letters to the Editor," *The Hindu*, January 17, 1978.
7. Lemery, M., *Histoire de l'Academie Royale des Sciences* (book), published in 1708.
8. Krebs, Martin, *Rekonvaleszentenharn zur Abschwaechung akuter Infectionen*, Monatzeitschrift fuer Kinderheilkunde, Vol. 82, 1940, pp. 1-8.
9. Krebs, Martin, *Masernabschwaechung durch Rekonvaleszentenharn*, Monatzeitschrift fuer Kinderheilkunde, Vol. 87, 1941, pp. 292-297.
10. Shankardevananda Saraswati, Swami, *Amaroli*, Bihar School of Yoga (Australia), 1978, p. 21.
11. Burzynski, Stanislaus R., et al., "Antineoplaston A in Cancer Therapy," *Physiology, Chemistry & Physics*, Vol. 9, 1977, p. 485.
12. Weissenborn, Gunther, et al., "Experience with Auto-Urotherapy," (letter), *Der Landarzt*, Vol. 41, No. 35, December 20, 1965, pp. 1520-1522.
13. Kolata, Gina, "Surgery on Fetuses Reveals They Heal Without Scars," *New York Times*, August 16, 1988, p. C1 & C3.
14. Ibid.
15. Staff Reporter, "Nun Aids the Infertile," source unknown at this time.
16. Smith, Homer W., "De Urina," *Journal of the American Medical Association*, Vol. 155, No. 10, July 3, 1954, pp. 899-902.

17. "Immuno-Tolerance: Historical Perspective," *Physician's Handbook*, 1982, p. 7.
18. Staff Reporter, "Factor S: Help for the Wee, Wee Hours," source unknown at this time.
19. Staff Reporter, untitled, *The Mother Earth News*, No. 80, March, 1983, p. 40.
20. Staff Reporter, "Auto-Urine," *Time of India*, May 6, 1982.
21. Tsuji, S., et al., "Isolation from Human Urine of a Polypeptide Having Marked Tuberculostatic Activity," *American Review of Respiratory Diseases*, Vol. 91, No. 6, June, 1965, pp. 832-838.
22. Palladino, Q., "Urine-Therapy, Drinking from Thine Own Cistern," *PWA Coalition Newsline*, Issue 37, October, 1988, pp. 41-44.
23. Kaye, Donald, "Antibacterial Activity of Human Urine," *Journal of Clinical Investigation*, Vol. 47, 1968, pp. 2374-2390.
24. Plesch, J., "Urine-Therapy," *Medical Press* (London), Vol. 218, August 6, 1947, pp. 128-133.
25. Lerner, A.M., et al., "Neutralizing Antibody to Polioviruses in Normal Human Urine," *Journal of Clinical Investigation*, Vol. 41, No. 4, April, 1962, pp. 805-815.
26. Palladino, Q., "Urine-Therapy, Drinking from Thine Own Cistern," *PWA Coalition Newsline*, Issue 37, October, 1988, pp. 41-44.
27. Kaye, Donald, "Antibacterial Activity of Human Urine," *Journal of Clinical Investigation*, Vol. 47, 1968, pp. 2374-2390.
28. Duncan, Charles H., "Autotherapy," *New York Medical Journal*, Dec. 21, 1921, p. 1279.
29. "Immuno-Tolerance: Historical Perspective," *Physician's Handbook*, 1982, p. 7.
30. Liao, Zenghua, et al., "Identification of a Specific Interleukin-1 Inhibitor in the Urine of Febrile Patients," *Journal of Experimental Medicine*, Rockefeller University Press, Vol. 159, January, 1984, pp. 126-136.
31. Staff Reporter, "Now Urine Business," *Hippocrates* (magazine), May, 1988.
32. Fischer, E., "Rectale Eigenurin-Behandlung des Schwangerenbrechens," *Medizinische Klinik*, Vol. 32, Sep. 18, 1936, pp. 1298-1299.

33. Herman, John R., "Autourotherapy," *New York State Journal of Medicine*, Vol. 80, No. 7, June, 1980, pp. 1149-1154.

34. Free, A.H., and Free, H.M., *Urinalysis in Clinical Laboratory Practice*, CRC Press, Cleveland, Ohio, 1975, pp. 13 & 17.

35. Davies Owens, "Youthful Uric Acid," *Omni*, October, 1982.

36. Bjornesjo, K.B., "On the Effect of Human Urine on Tubercle Bacilli: II The Tuberculostatic Effect of Various Urine Constituents," *Acta Scandinavica*, Vol. 25, No. 5, 1951, pp. 447-455.

37. Burzynski, Stanislaus R., et al., "Antineoplaston A in Cancer Therapy," *Physiology, Chemistry & Physics*, Vol. 9, 1977, p. 485.

38. Thompson, H.H., "H-11 for Cancer," *British Medical Journal*, July 31, 1943, p. 149.

39. Ollerenshaw, G.J.W., "Observations on Dosage of H-11 Extract," *Medical World*, London, Vol. 64, March 1, 1946, pp. 72-76.

40. Tanaka & Tuboi, title not yet known, Gann., 1940, Vol. 34, p. 346.

41. Shankardevananda Saraswati, Swami, *Amaroli*, Bihar School of Yoga (Australia), 1978, p. 21.

42. Ibid.

43. Lerner, A.M., et al., "Neutralizing Antibody to Polioviruses in Normal Human Urine," *Journal of Clinical Investigation*, Vol. 41, No. 4, April, 1962, pp. 805-815.

44. Hanson, Lars A., et al., "Characterization of Antibodies in Human Urine," *Journal of Clinical Investigation*, Vol. 44, No. 5, 1965, pp. 703-715.

45. Plesch, J., "Urine-Therapy," *Medical Press* (London), Vol. 218, August 6, 1947, pp. 128-133.

46. Sandweiss, D.J., et al., "The Effect of Urine Extracts on Peptic Ulcer," *American Journal of Digestive Diseases*, Vol. 8, No. 10, October, 1941, pp. 371-382.

47. Shankardevananda Saraswati, Swami, *Amaroli*, Bihar School of Yoga (Australia), 1978, p. 37.

48. Bjornesjo, K.B., "Tuberculostatic Factor in Normal Human Urine," *American Review of Tuberculosis*, Vol. 73, No. 6, June, 1956, p. 967.

49. Tsuji, S., et al., "Isolation from Human Urine of a Polypeptide Having Marked Tuberculostatic Activity," *American Review of Respiratory Diseases*, Vol. 91, No. 6, June, 1965, pp. 832-838.

50. James, John S., "DHEA: Mystery AIDS Treatment," *Aids Treatment News*, Issue 48, January 1, 1988, pp. 1-6.

51. Kent, Saul, "DHEA: Miracle Drug?," *Geriatrics*, Vol. 37, No. 9, 1982, pp. 157-161.

52. Tonasi, Thomas, et al., "Characteristics of an Immune System Common to Certain External Secretions," *Journal of Experimental Medicine*, Vol. 121, No. 1, January, 1965, p. 101-122.

53. Duncan, Charles H., "Autotherapy," *New York Medical Journal*, Vol. 96, 1912, pp. 1278-1283.

54. Schlegel, J.U., et al., "Bactericidal Effect of Urea," *Journal of Urology*, Vol. 86, No. 6, December, 1961, pp. 819-822.

55. Ibid.

56. Muldavin, Leon, et al., title not yet known, *The Lancet*, March 3, 1938, p. 549.

57. Bello, Eduardo, "The Original Therapy of Wounds with Urine, Practice Traditional with Peruvian Indians, Explained and Justified," *Revista Medica de Vera Cruz* (Mexico), Vol. 20, No. 4, April 1, 1940, pp. 3067-3071.

58. Bjorniesjo, K.B., "On the Effect of Human Urine on Tubercle Bacilli: II The Tuberculostatic Effect of Various Urine Constituents," *Acta Scandinavica*, Vol. 25, No. 5, 1951, pp. 447-455.

59. Myrvik, Q., et al., "Studies on the Tuberculoinhibitory Properties of Ascorbic Acid Derivatives and Their Possible Role in Inhibition of Tubercle Bacilli by Urine," *American Review of Tuberculosis*, Vol. 69, No. 3, March, 1954, pp. 406-418.

60. Desai, Paragji, D., *Shivambu Cure* (book), pp. 55-56.

61. Ibid., p. 22.

62. Shankardevananda Saraswati, Swami, *Amaroli*, Bihar School of Yoga (Australia), 1978, p. 21.

63. Duffy, M., et al., "Urokinase-Plasminogen Activator, A Marker for Aggressive Breast Carcinomas," *Cancer*, Vol. 62, No. 3, August 1, 1988, pp. 531-533.

64. Staff Writers, "Blood Clots: Legs and Lungs," *Harvard Medical School Health Letter*, Vol. 10, No. 3, January, 1985, p. 5.

65. Untitled, *Science Digest*, July, 1958.

66. Shankardevananda Saraswati, Dr. Swami, *Amaroli*, Bihar School of Yoga, Australia, 1978, p. 22.

67. Kimball, Ed, et al., "Interleukin-1 Activity in Normal Human Urine," source and date unknown at this time.

68. Oriel, G.H., "Some Observations on the Biochemistry of Asthma," *Guy's Hospital Report*, Vol. 79, 1929, pp. 480-490.

69. Stanley, E.R., et al., "Colony Stimulating Factor and the Regulation of Granulopoiesis and Macrophage Production," source and date unknown at this time.

70. Staff Reporter, "Factor S: Help for the Wee, Wee Hours," source and date unknown at this time.

71. Darley, W., et al., "Studies on Urinary Proteose; Skin Reactions and Therapeutic Applications in Hay Fever," *Annals of Internal Medicine*, Vol. 6, No. 3, 1932, pp. 389-399.

72. Herman, John R., "Autourotherapy," *New York State Journal of Medicine*, Vol. 80, No. 7, June, 1980, pp. 1149-1154.

73. Plesch, J., "Urine-Therapy," *Medical Press* (London), Vol. 218, August 6, 1947, pp. 128-133.

74. Duncan, Charles H., "Gonorrhea: Its Prevention andCure by Autotherapy," *Medical Record*, March 30, 1912, p. 614.

75. "Immuno-Tolerance: Historical Perspective," *Physician's Handbook*, 1982, p. 13.

76. Duncan, Charles H., "Gonorrhea: Its Prevention andCure by Autotherapy," *Medical Record*, March 30, 1912, p. 610.

77. Duncan, Charles H., "Autotherapy," *New York Medical Journal*, December 21, 1912, p. 1281.

78. Wilson, C.W.M., and Lewis, A., "Auto-Immune Therapy Against Human Allergic Disease: A Physiological Self Defense Factor," *Medical Hypothesis*, Vol. 12, 1983, p. 143.

79. Turner, M.W., and Rowe, D.S., "Characterization of Human Antibodies to Salmonella Typhi by Gelfiltration and Antigenic Analysis," *Immunology*, Vol. 7, 1964, p. 639.

80. Berger, R., Ainbender, E., Hodes, H.L., Zepp, H.D., and Hedvizy, M.M., "Demonstration of IgA Polio-Antibody in Saliva, Duodenal Fluid and Urine," *Nature*, Vol. 214, 1967, p. 420.

81. Turner, M.W., and Rowe, D.S., "Antibodies of IgA and IgC Class in Normal Human Urine," *Immunology*, Vol. 12, 1967, p. 689.

82. Bienenstock, J., and Tomasi, T.B., "γA Rheumatoid Factor in Urine," Proceedings from the 4th Pan-American Congress on Rheumatology, Mexico City, Mexico, 1967.

83. "Immuno-Tolerance: Historical Perspective," *Physician's Handbook*, 1982, p. 13.

84. Wilson, C.W.M., and Lewis, A., "Auto-Immune Therapy Against Human Allergic Disease: A Physiological Self Defense Factor," *Medical Hypothesis*, Vol. 12, 1983, pp. 143-158.

85. Ibid.

86. *Immuno-Tolerance: Historical Perspective*, Physician's Handbook, 1982, p. 4.

87. Krebs, Martin, "Rekonvaleszentenharn zur Abschwaechung akuter Infectionen," *Monatzeitschrift fuer Kinderheilkunde*, Vol. 82, 1940, pp. 1-8.

BOOKS ON URINE-THERAPY

Some of these books are out of print. The books marked with an asterisk (*) are easily available.

*1988 *The Miracles of Urine-Therapy* by Dr. Beatrice Bartnett and Margie Adelman, L.M.T., C.N., Water of Life Institute, P.O. Box 22-3543, Hollywood, Florida 33022-3543.

*1982 *Urine-Therapy: Self-Healing Through Intrinsic Medicine* by J. O'Quinn, Life Science Institute, P.O. Box 1057, Fort Pierce, Florida 33434.

1980 *The Lost Gospel of the Ages* by J.C. Androgeus, Life Science Institute, P.O. Box 1057, Fort Pierce, Florida 33434.

1979 *Siddhargal Kanda Siruneer Maruthuvam* by Dr. R. Manickavasagam, India.

1978 *Shivambu Kalpa* by Dr. Arthur Lincoln Pauls, England.

1978 *Miracles of Urine Therapy* by Dr. Mithal, India.

1978 *Amaroli* by Dr. Swami Shankardevan Saraswati, Bihar School of Yoga, Australia.

1973 *Manav Mootra* by Dr. R.M. Patel, India.

1969 *Auto-Urine Cure* by Kevlekar and Raghuvanshi, Shri Gajanan Book Depot, Kabutarkhana, Bhawani Shankar Road, Dadar, Bombay 28, India.

1950 *Eigenharnbehandlung* by Dr. Johann Abele, Karl F. Haug Verlag, Heidelberg, Germany.

*1944 *Water of Life* by John W. Armstrong, Health Science Press, 1 Church Path, Saffron Walden, Essex, England.

1918 *Autotherapy* by Dr. Charles Duncan, USA.

For a list of available books, tapes, and the *Lifestyle News*, our quaterly newsletter, please send a self-addressed, stamped envelope to:

> Lifestyle Institute
> P.O. Box 4735
> Ruidoso, NM 88345

Ruidoso Health Institute

Located in beautiful Ruidoso, New Mexico, the *Ruidoso Health Institute*, under the direction of Dr. Beatrice Bartnett, is offering quality alternative health care for today's health problems.

The Institute specializes in chronic and degenerative conditions such as

> Chronic Fatigue Syndrome
> Allergies & Asthma
> Environmental Sensitivities
> and many more

The treatments are specifically design to each individual patient. Some of the better known treatment protocols we use are

> NAET (Allergy Elimination Treatment)
> Enzyme Therapy
> Lymph Detoxification Therapy
> Auriculo Therapy
> Chiropractic and Naturopathic Medicine

Call us and see how we can help you.
Phone consultations with Dr. Bartnett are available.

Ruidoso Health Institute
1204 Mechem #10, Ruidoso, New Mexico, USA
(505) 258-3046

Lymph Detoxification Seminars

are offered throughout the US. These seminars are designed for bodyworkers and other professionals and are approved by the National Board of Massage Therapy for 12 CE's

Please call for schedule (505) 258-3046

Order Form

Please send me_____copies of the book

The Key to the Ear

Enclosed is a check or money order for $ 12.45 per book ($ 9.95 for the book plus $2.50 s/h). NM residents please add 6.9375% sales tax ($0.69 per book).

Name_____

Address_____

City, State_____ ZIP_____

send to: Lifestyle Institute
P.O. Box 4735
Ruidoso, NM 88345

- -

Order Form

Please send me_copies of the book

Peace Labyrinth - Sacred Geometry

Enclosed is a check or money order for $ 9.95 per book plus $2.50 s/h. NM residents please add 6.9375% sales tax ($0.69 per book).

Name _____

Address_____

City, State_____ ZIP_____

send to: Lifestyle Institute
P.O. Box 4735
Ruidoso, NM 88345

INDEX

About the Author

Dr. Beatrice Bartnett, D.C., N.D. was born and educated in Switzerland. Being exposed to alternative healing at an early age, it was only natural for her to enter the field of Naturopathy. After her studies in Germany, she practiced as a Naturopathic Physician in Switzerland.

In the early 1980's, Dr. Bartnett came to America to study Chiropractic. She holds a degree from Life Chiropractic College in Georgia. In 1987 she earned her Doctorate in Naturopathy.

A pioneer in alternative healing methods, especially Auto Therapies, Dr. Bartnett has done extensive research and has lectured in India, Europe, Central America, the Caribbean Islands, Canada and the USA. She has been on radio and television in several countries.

Dr. Bartnett has authored six books and numerous articles and pamphlets. One of the books has been translated into several languages. She is the editor of the quarterly newsletter publication, *Southern New Mexico Health Beat*, formerly the *Lifestyle News*. In 1991, Dr. Bartnett founded the Lifestyle Institute.

Dr. Bartnett practices at the *Ruidoso Health Institute* in New Mexico. She has developed a new approach to prevention and recovery of today's health conditions. It is a combination of nutrition, naturopathic bodywork, lymphdrainage, auriculotherapy, detoxification, stress control, exercise and body, mind and spirit balancing. She also specializes in Allergy Elimination with the NAET method. Because of her success and unique approach, Dr. Bartnett takes care of patients from all continents either in her practice or by phone.